# Galapagos Tortoise

Curious Kids Press

Please note:All Rights Reserved. No part of this publication may be reproduced in any form or by any means, including scanning, photocopying, or otherwise without prior written permission of the copyright holder. Copyright © 2014

# Galapagos Tortoise

There are hundreds of species of the tortoise. However, there is only one Galapagos Tortoise. Unlike turtles, the Galapagos Tortoise is a land-dwelling animal. It gets its name from the area it lives in. Like all tortoises, the Galapagos is a reptile. It appears to be almost ancient. In this book we are going to explore many things about this slow animal. We are going to discover where this creature lives, its extraordinary abilities and so much more. Read on to be totally amazed with this cool creature.

# Where in the World?

Did you know this tortoise gets its name from where it was found in abundance? Spanish explorers first found this tortoise on the Galapagos Islands. There were so many of them, the explorers named the tortoise after this area. Galapagos in Spanish means, tortoise.

# The Body of the Galapagos Tortoise

Did you know the Galapagos is the largest tortoise in the world? This reptile has a relatively long neck and a short tail. Males can weigh from 112 to 705 pounds (51 to 320 kilograms). Its shell alone takes up most of its weight. This tortoise can also measure around 4 feet long (1.2 meters).

# The Legs of the Galapagos Tortoise

Did you know the legs of some Galapagos tortoises are very thick and stumpy? Their leg are very strong. They need to be to hold up this reptile's tremendous weight. However, even though this tortoise has powerful legs, it likes to lie down. This helps it conserve energy.

# The Shell of the Galapagos Tortoise

Did you know the shell of this tortoise can look different depending on its habitat? The tortoises in the lush habitat have doomed shells. The tortoises living in sparser conditions have saddleback shells. These shells are also filled with honey-comb-like spaces. This makes it easier and lighter for the tortoise to haul around.

# The Skin of the Galapagos Tortoise

Did you know this reptile has tough skin ? The scaly skin on the Galapagos tortoises legs and head act as a layer of armor - it is very leathery and strong. It keeps this tortoise from getting injuries, like scrapes and cuts, while it is moving around.

# What a the Galapagos Tortoise Eats

Did you know this tortoise is a herbivore? This means it eats only plants. It will dine on prickly pear cactus and fruits, bromeliads, water ferns, leaves and grasses. It also has a tremendous ability to store water. This enables it to survive the long dry seasons.

# The Galapagos Tortoises Special Ability

Did you know this tortoise can move fast when it wants to? We may think all tortoises are slow. But the Galapagos Tortoise can move quite fast. It can travel up to 8 miles (13 kilometers) in two days. This is usually done in the breeding season when the male is looking for a mate.

# Male Galapagos Tortoises

Did you know the male Galapagos Tortoise will fight another male? The tortoises face each other with ferocious glares. They then open their mouths and stretch out their long necks. Whoevers neck is the longest wins. The loser pulls his head in with a noisy hiss and leaves.

# Galapagos Tortoise Mom

Did you know the female Galapagos only lays between 2 and 16 eggs? Mom tortoise digs a big hole to lay her eggs in. Once she is finished she covers the hole back up. The mother then leaves her eggs to hatch. This is done about 4 to 8 months later.

# Baby Galapagos Tortoises

Did you know it takes the baby tortoises about a month to dig out of their nest? The temperature of the nest will make the baby tortoises either boys or girls. Warm nests will produce more girl eggs, while cooler nest produce more boys. Baby tortoises are hunted by many predators.

# Predators of the Galapagos Tortoise

Did you know humans were the biggest predator to the Galapagos Tortoise? They were hunted for their meat and their shells. Also, humans introduced pigs, dogs, rats and goats to the Galapagos Islands. These species both hunted young tortoises and also ate the eggs and the tortoises food supply.

# Life of the Galapagos Tortoise

Did you know this tortoise can live to be 150 years-old? The Galapagos tortoise is very quiet, peaceful and lazy. It gets up in the morning to bask in the sun. After it has warmed up it will begin to forage for food. In the evening it settles down for the night among the shrubs or submerged in water.

# Speckled Tortoise

Did you know this is the smallest species of tortoise? This little guy is found in South Africa. It only grows to about 3.9 inches long (10 centimeters). It has a flattened shell with slightly serrated edges and hundreds of black spots all over it. This tortoise likes to hang out in rocky areas.

# Desert Tortoise

Did you know this tortoise has a high-domed shell? It has powerful legs and claws on its feet. It uses these to dig deep burrows. It likes to dine on vegetation, including annual wildflowers, grasses, new growth of selected shrubs, cacti and their flowers.

# Leopard Tortoise

Did you know this tortoise is found in the savannas of eastern and southern Africa? This tortoise gets its name from its beautifully printed shell. The leopard tortoise likes to eat prickly pears, succulents and thistles. It can live from 80 to 100 years-old.

# Quiz

# Question 1: What is the Spanish word for Tortoise?

# Answer 1: "Galapagos"

# Question 2: How much can the Galapagos Tortoise weigh in at?

**Answer 2: 705 pounds (320 kilograms)**

**Question 3: Is this tortoise a herbivore (plant-eater) or a carnivore (meat-eater)?**

# Answer 3: Herbivore

**Question 4: What does the tortoise's tough skin protect it from?**

# Answer 4: Scrapes and cuts

**Question 5: Where does the smallest tortoise species live?**

# Answer 5: South Africa

**Thank you for checking out another title from Curious Kids Press! Make sure to search "Curious Kids Press" on Amazon.com for many other great books.**